Acid Rain

Lucy Poddington

First published in 2006 by
Franklin Watts
338 Euston Road
London NW1 3BH

Franklin Watts Australia
Hachette Children's Books
Level 17/207 Kent Street
Sydney NSW 2000

This book is based on Our Planet in Peril: Acid Rain by Louise Petheram
© Franklin Watts 2002. It is produced for Franklin Watts by Painted Fish Ltd.
Designer: Rita Storey

Acknowledgements
The publishers would like to thank the following for permission to reproduce
photographs in this book.

Greg Abel/Environmental Images: 9bl; Martin Bond/Environmental Images: 28t;
Andrew Brown/Ecoscene: 9t, 17t; Graham Burns/Environmental Images: 11br;
John Corbett/Ecoscene: 12t; Corbis: 23t; Colin Cuthbert/SPL: 8t; Stephen Dalton/
NHPA: 19t; Ecoscene: fr cover, 22b; Mark Edwards/Still Pictures: 6t, 19b; Mary Evans
PL: 10b; Mark Fallander/Environmental Images: 14cl; © FSC: 17b; Dylan Garcia/
Still Pictures: 27b; Don Gray/Photofusion: 15t; Nick Hawkes/Ecoscene: 14tr; Mike
Jackson/Still Pictures: 5tl; Jonathan Kaplan/Still Pictures: 14-15b; Yoram Lehmann/
Still Pictures: 11tr; Charlotte MacPherson/Environmental Images: 16b; Chris Martin/
Environmental Images: 4c; Rick Miller/Agstock/SPL: 20-21; Sally Morgan/Ecoscene:
17c; Eddie Mulholland/ Reuters/Popperfoto: 11bl; Juan Carlos Munoz/Still Pictures:
7t; Trevor Perry/Environmental Images: 12-13b, 21bl; Melanie Peters/Ecoscene: 29c;
Ray Pforter/ Still Pictures: 22tl; Richard Pike/Still Pictures: 26b; Charlie Pye-Smith:
28-29; Harmut Schwarz/Still Pictures: 23c; R. Sorensen & J.Olsen/NHPA: 18t;
Tek Image/SPL: 25t; Wolk-UNEP/Still Pictures: 4-5b.

A CIP catalogue record for this book
is available from the British Library

ISBN 0 7946 6514 9
Dewey classification: 363.738'6
Printed in Dubai

Contents

The acid rain problem   4

What is acid rain?   6

Measuring acid rain   8

What causes acid rain?   10

Pollution on the move   12

Breathing problems   14

Forests in trouble   16

Lakes and streams   18

Plants and food crops   20

Buildings and bridges   22

Around the world   24

The solution so far   26

What about the future?   28

Further information   30

Glossary   31

Index   32

Words printed in *italic* are explained in the glossary.

The acid rain problem

Scientists have discovered that a type of *pollution*, called acid rain, has damaged trees and buildings in some places. The word *acid* means sour. Foods such as lemon juice and vinegar are acids. Acid rain is rain that contains more acid than usual.

These trees have been harmed by acid rain.

Damage to stone and metal

Acid rain wears away things made of stone and metal. Many old buildings have carvings made of stone. Acid rain wears away the stone so that the carvings become less clear. Acid rain also means that metal bridges and railway lines need to be repaired more often. It turns cars rusty so they do not last as long.

Damage to plants and animals

When acid rain soaks into the soil, it puts acid into the soil. This can stop trees and plants from growing properly. In Europe and North America, large areas of forest have been damaged in this way. Acid rain also puts acid into lakes and streams. This is harmful to fish.

Acid rain makes vehicles turn rusty more quickly.

Health problems

In places where there is acid rain, there are tiny pieces of acid in the air. When people breathe in the air, the acid causes breathing problems and illnesses such as *asthma*. People with these problems often take medicines and they may need to have time off work or school.

Acid in the air makes breathing problems worse.

◆ How you can help

Some acid rain is caused by power stations which make electricity. You can help the problem by using less electricity. Remember to switch off computers and turn out the lights when you leave a room.

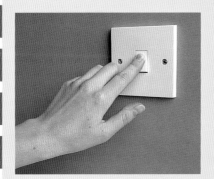

Using less electricity helps to solve the acid rain problem.

What is acid rain?

Tiny droplets of water move around in the air.

The air is a mixture of *gases*. There are tiny *particles* of water in the air, called water vapour. Harmful gases can mix with the water vapour and make it more acidic than usual. When the acidic water vapour turns into raindrops and falls to the ground, it is called acid rain.

The causes of acid rain

Acid rain is caused by gases which pollute the air. Factories and cars give off these gases when they burn *fuel* to make *energy*. The gases come out of the factory chimneys and car exhaust pipes. When these gases mix with the air, they dirty the air and create pollution. This makes acid rain.

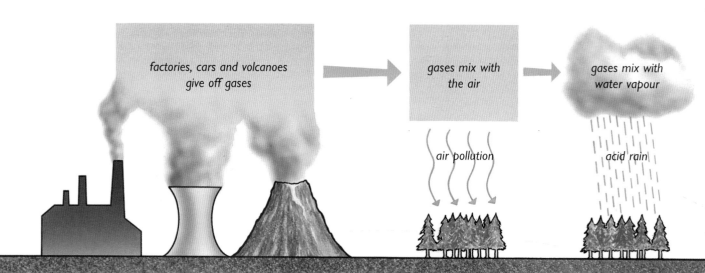

factories, cars and volcanoes give off gases

gases mix with the air

air pollution

gases mix with water vapour

acid rain

Volcanoes

When a volcano erupts, it gives off a mixture of gases. Some of these gases are the same as those that come from factories and from car exhausts. The gases cause acid rain near the volcano.

Erupting volcanoes give off gases which cause acid rain.

Acid in the air

Acid in the air causes the same problems as acid rain. The wind blows the acidic air to different places. The acid lands on the ground, on buildings and on vehicles. This causes the same damage as acid rain.

◆ Problem solving

In the 1980s and 1990s, new laws made the *fumes* from car exhausts safer. Today all new cars in Europe and the USA have a 'catalytic converter' which changes the harmful gases into safer ones. This means that less air pollution and acid rain comes from exhausts.

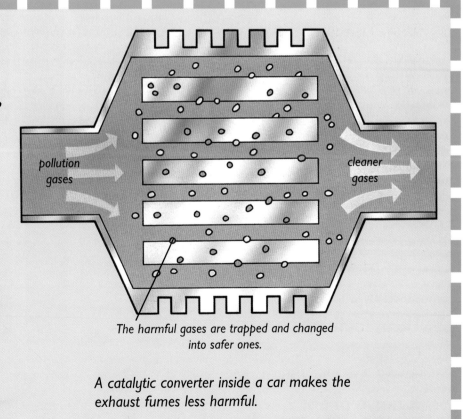

pollution gases

cleaner gases

The harmful gases are trapped and changed into safer ones.

A catalytic converter inside a car makes the exhaust fumes less harmful.

Measuring acid rain

Scientists test rainwater to see how acidic it is. They also measure how much pollution is in the air. This tells them how serious the problem of acid rain is. It also helps them to find out where the acid pollution is coming from.

A scientist uses a pH meter to test the amount of acid in the rain.

Acids and alkalis

Acids, such as lemon juice and vinegar, taste sour. *Alkalis* are the opposite of acids. Soap and toothpaste are alkalis. Acids and alkalis are measured using *pH numbers*. Acids have pH numbers less than 7. Alkalis have pH numbers greater than 7. A strong acid is pH 1 or 2 and a strong alkali is pH 13 or 14. Something that is neither an acid nor an alkali is called neutral. It has a pH of 7.

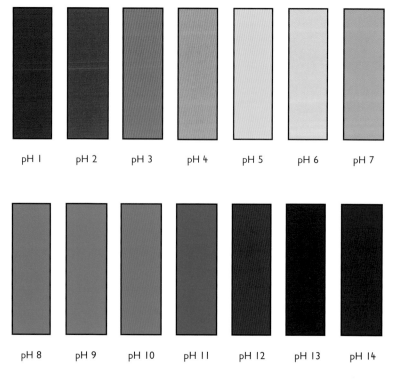

Universal Indicator Paper changes colour to show whether something is acid or alkali.

Measuring acid pollution

Even when the air is clean, it can still contain harmful acid pollution. Scientists collect air samples from different places. They use machines to find out which gases are mixed with the air. Scientists also collect rainwater and use a pH meter to find the rain's pH value.

Limestone is an alkali. It makes acid rain less harmful.

This machine collects air samples. Scientists will test the samples for air pollution.

Measuring acid in soil

Acid rain puts acid into the soil. To find out how much acid there is in soil, you can use a pH indicator to see what colour it turns. When acid mixes with an alkali, it becomes weaker, or less acidic. *Limestone* is an alkali. So, when acid rain falls on limestone, the acid becomes less harmful.

◆ Science in action

Collect rainwater samples from different places near your home. Use Universal Indicator Paper (available from your school or from chemistry sets) to measure how acidic your rainwater samples are.

What causes acid rain?

Burning fuel to heat our homes causes acid rain.

When fuel is burned, it causes acid rain. Fuels such as coal, oil and natural gas are burned to power cars and to make electricity in power stations. These fuels are called *fossil fuels*. They were formed millions of years ago from dead plants and animals. Different types of fuel cause different amounts of acid rain.

The history of acid rain

Acid rain was first formed when factories started to burn fuel to power their machines. In Britain, this happened at the start of the Industrial Revolution, in about 1750. But people did not learn about acid rain until scientists discovered the problem in the late 20th century.

In Britain in 1750, factories like these caused the first acid rain.

Fossil fuels and acid rain

In the USA, scientists have found that most of the gases that cause acid rain come from burning fossil fuels in power stations, factories and people's homes. The rest of the gases come from vehicles that burn petrol or diesel.

Factories and power stations that burn coal give off many of the gases that cause acid rain.

Solving the problem

When scientists discovered acid rain, they realised that we needed to put fewer harmful fumes into the air. Governments worked with factories and businesses to make new laws. It took a long time to decide on the new laws, because the ways of producing fewer waste gases are expensive to put into action.

Politicians have made laws to help solve the problem of acid rain.

◆ Problem solving

Power stations can clean the gases in their chimneys to make them safer before they mix into the air. Some power stations use natural gas as fuel instead of coal. This produces much less air pollution. Electricity can also be made using energy from the Sun, waves or wind. This does not produce any harmful gases.

These wind turbines use wind power to make electricity.

Pollution on the move

Acid rain is formed in places where many people live, because this is where most factories and cars are found. However, the pollution that causes acid rain can travel hundreds of kilometres, away from towns and cities and into the countryside.

Acid rain can travel from cities to the countryside.

How air pollution moves around

The gases that cause acid rain are very light, so they are easily carried by the wind. In strong winds, the gases can travel a long way. The warmer the air temperature is, the easier it is for gases in the air to move around.

Tall chimneys

Factories have tall chimneys so that smoke and other gases are let out high in the air. The wind carries away the fumes and spreads them out over a large area. This makes the fumes thinner and less harmful. It is safer for the people who live near the factory.

The wind carries smoke away from factories.

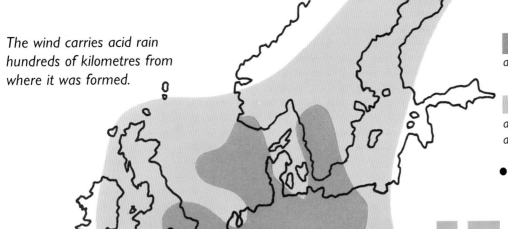

The wind carries acid rain hundreds of kilometres from where it was formed.

areas with strong acid rain

areas with medium-strength acid rain

• countries which produce a large amount of air pollution

wind direction

Science in action

This investigation shows how pollution moves in water. Gases in the air move in the same way.

Ask an adult to help you to mix some hot water and food colouring in a jar. This is your 'pollution'. Fill another jar with hot water. Fill a third jar with cold water. Dip a straw in the 'pollution' and place your finger over the end. Put the straw into each jar and slowly let out some 'pollution' into the bottom by lifting your finger. Watch how the 'pollution' moves.

Where does the acid rain end up?

The wind often blows in the same direction. This means that acid rain often travels on the same path. Many countries in central Europe have high levels of acid rain, even if they do not produce much themselves. A lot of acid rain in Canada comes from the USA.

Breathing problems

When people breathe in polluted air, it causes damage to their lungs. The more pollution there is in the air, the more harm it causes to people's bodies.

You can see this smoke in the air, but often air pollution is invisible.

Acid particles cause breathing problems when they enter the lungs.

Breathing polluted air

Polluted air contains tiny pieces of acid, called acid particles. When people breathe in the polluted air, these particles enter their lungs. This damages the lungs. It causes illnesses such as *bronchitis* and asthma. People with these illnesses have breathing problems and can even die from them.

Trapped pollution

In some cities, polluted air becomes trapped near the ground. It hangs over the city like fog. This happens when a layer of warmer air higher up stops the polluted air from rising and moving away. Mexico City, in Mexico, and Tokyo, in Japan, sometimes have this problem. The air pollution causes health problems for the people who live there.

These children are walking to school with an adult.
This way of travelling does not cause any air pollution.

◆ **How you can help**

If you travel by bus or train instead of by car, you are helping to cut down on air pollution. Walking and cycling produce no pollution at all. Find out if your school has a 'walking bus' which lets you walk to school safely with an adult.

Towns and cities

People who live in towns and cities are more likely to have breathing problems than people who live in the countryside. This is because towns and cities have more factories and more traffic which give off the harmful gases. Children who live near busy roads may have asthma caused by the traffic fumes.

Air pollution in cities can look like a layer of fog.

Forests in trouble

In 1984, scientists did tests on trees in the Black Forest in Germany. They discovered that almost half the trees were damaged by acid rain. Trees in the USA, Canada and northern Europe were damaged, too.

Damaged forests

In the damaged forests, some trees died and others lost their leaves. Scientists did tests on the air, water and soil and found that acid rain was the problem.

Acid rain and trees

Trees need food from the soil, called *nutrients*. When acid rain soaks into the soil, it takes away some of the nutrients. This makes the trees weaker and more likely to get diseases.

Acid rain has made these trees lose their branches and leaves.

Trees on mountains

Acid rain causes more damage to trees that are high up on mountains. Scientists think this is because trees on mountains often have clouds of mist around them. Acid in the mist damages the leaves and makes the trees weaker.

It is difficult for trees to grow on mountains because there is less air. Acid rain makes it even more difficult for them to grow there.

Different soils

Some forests are better at surviving acid rain than others. Different types of soil can be acid or alkali. The stronger the acid in the soil, the harder it is for trees to grow. Trees that grow in acidic soil may die when acid rain puts even more acid into the soil. Trees that grow in alkali soil are more likely to survive because the acid is weakened.

Alkali soil weakens the acid in the rain and the trees stay healthy.

◆ How you can help

Forests that have been damaged by acid rain need time to recover. When you buy things made from wood, look for the Forest Stewardship Council (FSC) label. This means that the wood comes from healthy forests.

FSC

Lakes and streams

This lake in Norway is clear blue because very few animals and plants live in it. They have been killed by acid rain.

Acid is found in lakes and streams when acid rain falls into them. It also happens when acidic water drains into the lakes and streams through the soil. Sometimes acid rain picks up poisons from the soil and washes them into lakes, too.

Acid lakes

Most lakes and streams have a pH number between 6 and 8. In some parts of North America, many lakes have a pH below 5 because acid rain has made them acidic. Lakes in mountain areas may contain more acid than usual during storms, when heavy rain falls into the lakes. Lakes also become more acidic in spring, when the snow melts and extra water flows into them.

Water creatures

Acid in lakes and streams makes fish and other water animals unhealthy. Fish eggs may not hatch and if they do, the young fish may not grow properly. When the acid in the water is too strong, the creatures die out altogether. This is a problem for other animals that usually eat these creatures.

Frogspawn may not survive if acid rain falls into ponds.

Getting back to normal

When acid rain stops falling, the lakes and streams can recover and the water creatures may come back. This is happening in some lakes and streams, but it takes a long time.

below pH 4.0		no living things survive
pH 4.0		only frogs survive
pH 4.5		trout and other fish die
pH 5.0		mayflies die, fish eggs do not survive
pH 5.5		water snails die

◆ Problem solving

If an alkali is put into a lake, the acid in the lake becomes weaker and less harmful. People sometimes put limestone (an alkali) into lakes to help water animals survive. This works for a short time, but it is very expensive. It is not long before acid rain makes the lake acidic again.

This helicopter is dropping limestone into a lake. The limestone makes the acid in the lake less harmful.

Plants and food crops

Acid rain harms many plants, not just trees. Acid damages the leaves of plants, but the biggest problem is when acid rain soaks into the soil and makes the soil acidic. This takes away nutrients from the soil so that plants cannot grow properly. Many farmers treat their crops to help them survive acid rain.

Acid rain on leaves

Leaves have a tough, waxy surface which protects them from diseases. When acid rain falls on leaves, it damages the waxy surface. There are tiny holes in the surface which let in gas from the air and allow the plant to make food. Damage from acid rain blocks the holes and so the plant cannot make as much food.

tough, waxy surface

holes let in gas from the air

veins carry water through the leaf

Acid rain damages the surface of the leaf, so the plant is less likely to survive.

Farmers' crops

Acid rain takes away nutrients from the soil, so farmers put *fertilisers* on their crops to help them grow. When there is too much acid in the soil, farmers spray it with an alkali to weaken the acid.

Fertilisers help food crops to grow in acidic soil.

A few plants, such as cotton grass, grow well in acidic soil.

Acidic soil

Most plants do not grow well when there is a lot of acid in the soil. The acid makes the roots of the plants weaker. When seeds land on acidic soil, it is harder for them to grow into new plants.

◆ Science in action

Strong acid rain has the same pH as vinegar. Try this experiment with three trays of cress. Each day, water Tray 1 with tap water, Tray 2 with an equal mix of vinegar and tap water, and Tray 3 with vinegar. Give the same amount of liquid to each tray.

Tray 1
tap water

Tray 2
tap water
and vinegar

Tray 3
vinegar

Which tray of cress grows best?

Buildings and bridges

Acid rain wears away features on statues.

Acid rain harms many other things besides plants and animals. It can also damage stone buildings and metal bridges. Just as with trees, crops and lakes, the stronger the acid, the more damage it causes.

Acid rain on stone

Many beautiful buildings and statues are made from stone, such as marble or limestone. These stones are easy to carve into different shapes. Over time, the stone slowly wears away and the shapes become harder to recognise. Acid rain makes the stone wear away faster. Acid in the air can also damage stone. This is happening at the pyramids in Egypt.

This ancient stone figure is at the bottom of a pyramid in Egypt. It has been damaged by acid in the air.

Acid rain on metal

Metals such as iron and steel turn rusty when they get wet. Rust wears away the metal and makes it weaker. When acid rain falls on metal bridges and railway lines, they turn rusty much faster than usual and they have to be repaired more often.

In places where there is acid rain, metal bridges turn rusty quickly.

Protecting metal

People paint metal to stop it from turning rusty. If acid rain damages the paint, the metal can be repainted. But stone carvings cannot usually be painted, so the damaged parts are replaced with new stone.

New cars have special paint which is not easily damaged by acid rain.

◆ Science in action

Fill two jars with tap water. Then fill another two jars with vinegar. Take two pieces of chalk (a kind of limestone) and put one in a jar of water. Put the other in a jar of vinegar. Now take two 'copper' coins and drop one in the second jar of water. Drop the other in the second jar of vinegar. Leave them for two days. What has happened?

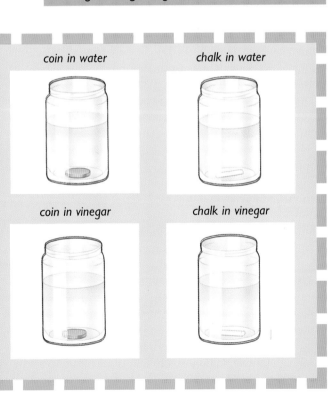

coin in water

chalk in water

coin in vinegar

chalk in vinegar

Around the world

Acid rain does not happen all over the world. Some countries produce a lot of the pollution that causes acid rain. Other countries produce very little pollution. The amount of acid rain in different places depends on things such as weather and how many factories are nearby.

The places coloured red produce the most acid rain pollution.

The places coloured blue have been harmed by acid rain.

Which places have the most problems?

Scientists do not know exactly which places have the most damage from acid rain because they are still doing tests to find out more. So far, scientists have discovered these facts:

• In 1984 in central Europe, almost half of the trees in some forests had been damaged by acid rain.
• In the eastern USA, acid pollution has harmed trees, fish and crops.
• Over 80% of people in Canada live in places which have problems caused by acid rain.

Working together

In the 1970s, scientists started to study the problem of acid rain. They discovered that some of the countries that have acid rain did not produce the acid rain themselves. So, countries needed to work together to solve the problem. Today, scientists from different countries tell each other what they find out. Politicians from around the world also work together to make plans that everyone is happy with.

Scientists around the world are working together to solve the problem of acid rain.

◆ How you can help

A lot of fuel is used to make plastic packaging for food. When you go shopping, try to buy food that has only the packaging it really needs. By doing this, you will cut down on pollution and help to solve the problem of acid rain.

Fuel is burned to make plastic packaging for food. This makes the acid rain problem worse.

The solution so far

In the late 1970s and early 1980s, people started trying to produce less acid rain to stop the damage it was causing. Scientists said that if this was not done, the problem of acid rain would become worse and worse. The way to produce less acid rain is to make cars, factories and power stations give off less gas that pollutes the air.

Controlling fumes from cars

Nearly all cars use petrol or diesel as fuel. They all give off some harmful gas, but old cars give off the most. In the 1980s and 1990s, governments made new laws to stop cars from giving off so many fumes. Now all cars have to be tested each year. If they give off too much harmful gas, they must be repaired.

Cars have to be tested every year to see how many harmful gases they give off.

Better power stations

Power stations that burn coal pollute the air and cause large amounts of acid rain. There are three ways to make power stations produce less pollution. Firstly, power stations can burn cleaner coal, which gives off less harmful gas. Secondly, power stations can clean the waste gases before they come out of the chimney into the air. Thirdly, we can build new power stations which use natural gas or *nuclear power* instead of coal.

◆ Problem solving

Governments in Europe and the USA have made laws to control the amount of harmful gas in the air. Scientists are learning more about acid rain and finding new ways to solve the problem. They tell the governments whether the laws are working, or if they need to be changed.

Nuclear power stations do not burn coal, so they do not cause acid rain. However, they produce waste that is very dangerous in other ways.

What about the future?

A thick material called insulation helps to trap heat in houses so it takes less energy to heat the house.

Many places have been damaged by acid rain. In the last 20 years, a lot of these places have started to recover. We do not know if we will ever stop acid rain altogether. Governments and businesses need to keep working together to solve the problem. But we can all help make a difference, if we think carefully about the things we buy and things we do.

Cleaner energy

There are ways of making electricity that do not produce the gases that cause acid rain. One such way is nuclear power. Electricity can also be made using the power of the Sun, wind or waves. Using wind power is cheaper than burning fossil fuels as well as cleaner.

This dam uses water power to make electricity. It does not give off any harmful gases so it does not cause acid rain.

Acid rain and global warming

The things we are doing to help the acid rain problem may be making *global warming* worse. Global warming is caused by gases in the air, called greenhouse gases, which trap heat from the Sun and make the air warmer. The gases that cause acid rain may bounce back some of the Sun's heat and help to stop the Earth from warming up.

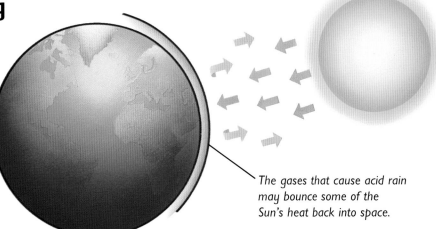

The gases that cause acid rain may bounce some of the Sun's heat back into space.

Some scientists think the gases that cause acid rain help to stop the Earth from warming up.

◆ How you can help

You can help to save energy by recycling paper, glass and metal cans. It takes less fossil fuel to recycle these things than to make new ones. The less fuel we use, the less pollution and acid rain we produce.

When you recycle your rubbish, you are helping to solve the problem of acid rain.

Government action

The government of the USA has set a target for cutting down on the gases that cause acid rain. Less and less harmful gas will be given off every year until 2010. Many countries around the world are doing the same. They hope that in 2010 they will produce half as much harmful gas as they did in 1980.

Further information

There are websites where you can find out more about the topics in this book.

http://www.ec.gc.ca/acidrain
This is the Environment Canada website which has lots of facts about acid rain.

http://www.ace.mmu.ac.uk/kids/index.html
Here you can find information, games and puzzles about acid rain and other pollution.

http://www.fsc-uk.org
This website tells you more about the Forest Stewardship Council and how it helps to save forests.

http://www.greenpeace.org.uk
The Greenpeace website has information about energy, pollution and forests.

http://www.walkingbus.com/index.htm
Here you can find out about walking buses. The kids' zone has advice on air pollution, recycling and saving energy.

http://www.wwf.org.uk/gowild
This World Wildlife Fund website has quizzes and information about pollution.

http://www.kidsplanet.org
At the Kids' Planet website, you can learn more about animals, the environment and how to save energy.

Glossary

acid
Something which has a pH number of less than 7. Lemon juice and vinegar are weak acids.

alkali
Something which has a pH number greater than 7. Soap and toothpaste are alkalis.

asthma
An illness which causes breathing problems.

bronchitis
An infection of the lungs which makes people cough.

energy
The power which makes people and machines move, or provides light and heat.

fertilisers
The substances that are put onto soil to help plants grow.

fossil fuels
The fuels made from the bodies of animals and plants that died millions of years ago. Coal, oil and natural gas are fossil fuels.

fuel
Something that gives off heat and energy when it burns.

fumes
Harmful or unpleasant gases, such as the gases from car exhaust pipes.

gas
A substance that is neither a liquid nor a solid. The air is a mixture of gases.

global warming
The warming up of the air around the Earth, over many years. It is caused by gases in the air which trap heat from the Sun.

limestone
A kind of rock which is an alkali. Chalk is a type of limestone.

nuclear power
A way of producing electricity that does not use fossil fuels.

nutrients
Substances that plants and animals need to grow and stay healthy.

particles
Very small pieces of something.

pH numbers
A set of numbers (0–14) for showing whether something is acid or alkali, and how strong it is.

pollution
Dirt or harmful substances in the air, water or soil.

Index

air 5, 6, 7, 8, 9, 11, 12, 13, 14, 15, 16, 20, 22, 26, 27, 29, 31
alkalis 8, 9, 17, 19, 21, 31
animals 4, 10, 18, 19, 22, 31
asthma 5, 14, 15, 31

breathing problems 5, 14–15, 31
buildings 4, 7, 22–23

cars 4, 6, 7, 10, 12, 15, 23, 26, 31

electricity 5, 10, 11, 28, 31
energy 6, 11, 28, 29, 31

factories 6, 7, 10, 11, 12, 15, 24, 26
farmers 20, 21
fish 4, 19, 24
forests 4, 16–17, 24
fossil fuels 10, 11, 28, 29, 31
fuel 6, 10, 11, 25, 26, 28, 29, 31

gases 6, 7, 9, 11, 12, 13, 15, 20, 26, 27, 28, 29, 29, 31
global warming 29, 31

lakes 4, 18–19, 22, 24
laws 7, 11, 26, 27
limestone 9, 19, 22, 31

metal 4, 22, 23, 29

nuclear power 27, 28, 31
nutrients 16, 20, 21, 31

pH numbers 8, 9, 18, 19, 21, 31
plants 4, 10, 18, 20–21, 22, 31
power stations 5, 10, 11, 26, 27

recycling 29

soil 4, 7, 9, 16, 17, 18, 20, 21, 24, 31
stone 4, 22, 23
Sun 11, 28, 29

trees 4, 16, 17, 20, 22, 24

volcanoes 7

wind 7, 11, 12, 13, 28